Happiest* Time of the Year

T. Vorreyer

BookLeaf Publishing

India | USA | UK

Presentation by *BookLeaf Publishing*

Web: www.bookleafpub.com

E-mail: info@bookleafpub.com

ISBN: 9789357214858

First edition 2022

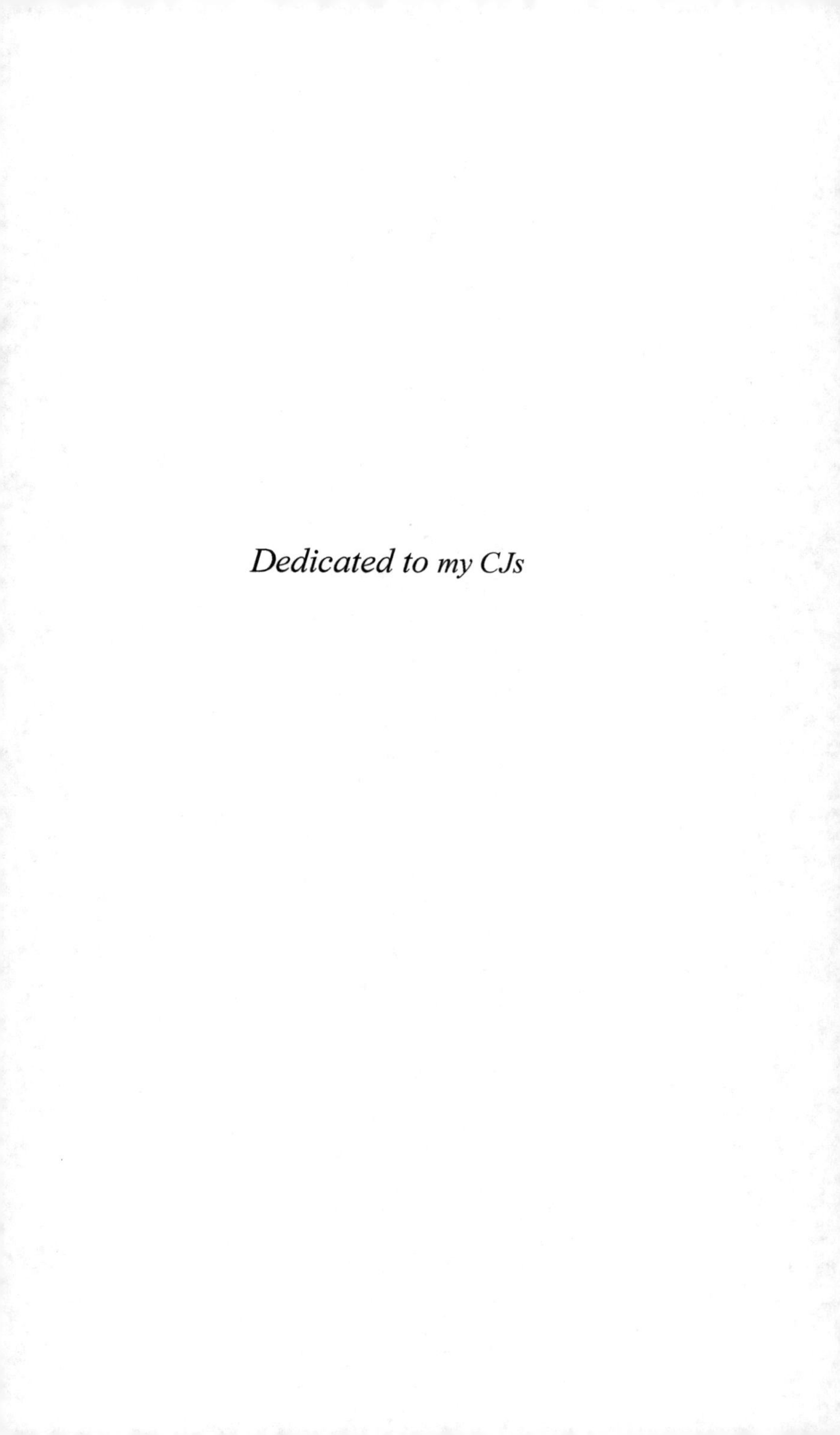

Dedicated to my CJs

ACKNOWLEDGEMENT

Thank you Taylor for always pushing me to write, thank you to my therapist for guiding me through this healing journey of mine, and lastly, thank you to my unbelievably supportive husband.

Happy Monday!

It's an oxymoron,
to wish someone a
Happy Monday -
I have yet to know of
a human soul who
has enjoyed a
Monday,
especially one this close
to "fuck it, it's Christmas".

But, I guess I haven't met
everyone.

Self-Awareness

Tell us what it is like to feel: *human.*
No, not the emotions –
The sensation.

Explain how there are waves beneath your chest
Crashing and Thrashing about your rib cage.
Paint us stories of when bricks of sand
Filled your limbs during a deep slumber –
Then your body turned to ice and then fire, all at
once
And all over.

For being human isn't just experiencing *Joy* or
Fear –
It is recognizing the storm inside yourself
And giving it a name.

What is in a Name?

3

To fulfill my name's prophecy,
I must not be the atheist that I am -
to be the nationality of my surname
at birth, I must pray for the sins
of the people before me -
to live life with my maiden name,
I must always be ready with
an explanation -
to hear my name called out
correctly for the first time,
I must have married the right man.

Or the syllables that contain
my name speak riddles rather -
all bringing you one step closer
to the person who answers.

Elemental Familiarity

Cascading waters once flowed
forward - a waterfall,
But pollution dyed it all black –
I built a popsicle stick dam
To keep the dark water at bay.

Yet, you wield a hammer,
Excavating my concrete
For diamonds – Unable to
Understand the nature
Of the the makeshift wall.
How do you juxtapose
A dam for a mine?
Far be it for me,
The damn architect,
To explain my work.

Go ahead, be my guest,
Clobber away for
I do not mind –
When the dam breaks,
I will live but
You'll surely drown.

Mother

5

Her – She's
Comatose inside the body
She was birthed into.
As she slumbers,
Her Banshee lives freely -
Shrieking and keening
In her delight.
       Once during a
       Red moon, I saw her
       Stir restlessly behind her eyes –
But I can no longer bring
Myself to search those
Copper encrusted caramel
Portals anymore,
For that is undoubtably
Where the Banshee keeps
Her knives.

Am I Allowed to be Angry?

As an adult
female -
an intellectual -
Do those attributes,
additive adjectives,
give me permission
for fury?
Or have I been forged
to only feel fear?

How am I
allowed to emote?

I Will No Longer Give You Energy

I will no longer fill your hunger
for control
for power.
I will no longer fear
your anger because
my fury has become a monster -
Sent to destroy your
castle upon the clouds.
Yet, your army planned for
Me - fueling their fires
with my fight.
So, I'll be on my way, to
extinguish the dying flame.
Find another source
Elsewhere -
someplace
far away from here.

Late December Nights

The streets are gray
reflective,
like a lead pencil tip -

Catch me,
I'm dizzy-
unable to see
even with my eyes
wide open.

Take me,
I'm not me tonight -
Let's go to the place
we always go
when she's in control.

Forget wishes,
forget dreams,
forget elevens -
I am the villain
in this book.

"You're In Rare Form Today"

The echo reverberates in my skull -
thin maroon lines along hip bone
ache in time with my beating
heart, a cowardly lion with sharp claws.
    rare form.
My aura radiates shame,
my fingernails soiled with
skin tissue and blood -
I would like to again
be small and unnoticeable.

Smoke Inhalation

Inhale –

I relish in the lung's constriction,
      A tight embrace from myself –
Emotive kink?
      Suffocated by self-love,
Dryly drowning in my addiction
To affection

– Exhale

Will It Hurt?

I would like a child, but
I do not want a baby.

Sure -
I'm not sure if I can handle
the pain that has produced
it's fair share of blood curdling screams,
the natural process of splitting open
from the bottom up -
but there's drugs for that.
What rattles my ribs,
nags at my noggin, and
gasses my guts is
the knowledge of
History - Memories
of the mothers who came before,
and the irrevocable terror
of it repeating.

I'm Realizing Now

Since moving into the driver's seat
of my life, I've noticed the following:

The gearshift sticks, often getting stuck on
reverse.
The steering wheel burns my hands, I have to
wear gloves.
The car has become a mess, as if I were
homeless and living inside.
There's certainly no heated seats, and the AC is
broken.
The mileage is low but the wear and tear is high.

I am not sure, sitting captain, that I know how to
drive at all.

(No) Boundaries

My neighbor visits
expectedly unexpectedly
often enough for
the other neighbors
to understandably assume
we've become polygamous…
        but
in our joint cowardice –
we live wondrously
deliciously
devotedly
impenetrably…
monogamous.

Salty

I stew in a pot of my own
melancholy -
replaying memories upside down,
pretending I'm unfractured -
underwhelmed,
undercooked.

Directions say to add seasoning...
    but, I'm white.

Do You Remember Being Diabolical?

Two words
Would turn any red headed human into a
Saint-
I'm sorry.

The vernacular part of my fault vocabulary-
These three syllables direct my show,
Hire the leads, and block the choreography
perfectly.
I'm sorry.

My Canadian "Eh",
I finish my sentences with
The flourish used only in grieving guilt:
I'm. Sorry.

I am.
I have one thousand sympathies to
my childhood that ended
sooner rather than later,
One million apologies that I kept the blinders on
for so long,
An infinite sorrows for the woman
I will never be thanks to the

woman before me,
          chronologically and metaphorically
speaking.

To you, to myself, to the world:
I am sorry
That I refuse to remove
From my vocabulary
The two words
That could save or curse me:

I. Am. Sorry.
I. Am. Not. Sorry.

Memories Lie

17

I loath those stories -
the ones with compromised credibility,
with realistically unreliable narrators
for it spreads the adhesive
while I stack brick after brick
upon my fragile wall.
If God forgets - then
who remembers?

If Only The Third Eye Opened

If only she could see today,
Would she have had more courage?
Would she have cut into skin deeper?
Would she have changed for the better?
Would it have mattered at all?

Does anyone care?
Should anyone care?

If it weren't for the logistics of it all,
Would my demise have been that bad?

Do you ever wish you remained
A Ghost?

Written in the Stars

She was a teenage
Scorpio mother with an aged
Capricorn daughter –
Their fates doomed
By the stars from the start.

She raised her mother
Until she birthed another, a
Libra baby boy –
There were diapers to
change and growth markers to chart.

He watched his sister
Put herself first, his eyes
Watering as she walked out –
Envy eventually turning into
Respect for the one who followed her heart…

and listened to her head.

Lucky Penny

Wouldn't it be most humorous
if, after picking up a stray penny
off of the sidewalk -
heads up, of course -
the deadliest disease is
transmitted to the
coin collector?

Call it a damned finders fee.

Glass & Mirrors

Velvet brown corduroy eyes
Sing in harmony back at me –
Is this confidence or contentment?
Are they one in the same?
       Or
Is this narcissism romanticized?
Is it fitting that I cannot decide,
For the girl looking back at me
Does not want to know.

Anonymous Amen

Words the color of Merlot –
twinkling like Christmas lights,
hung with good Christian care – (OPEN)
for this church is where I go
for peace on the
sabbath day.

I hope for forgiveness

      Nay –
I pray.

Holy art thou –
thy airplane bottles
that fit within thine pocket
so well.
Praise be Jesus –
the savior
who works behind the
counter, supplying his disciples
with the blood of his body.
Say you will love us
the same tomorrow.

      Please?